TEAMBUILDING

TEAMBUILDING
A Practical Guide

Alastair Fraser and Suzanne Neville

The Industrial Society

First published in 1993 by
The Industrial Society
Robert Hyde House
48 Bryanston Square
London W1H 7LN
Telephone: 071-262 2401

© *The Industrial Society 1993*

ISBN 0 85290 881 4

British Library Cataloguing-in-Publication Data.
A catalogue record for this book is available from the
British Library.

Typeset by: The Midlands Book Typesetting Company
Printed by: Cromwell Press
Cover Design: Pylon

Text illustrations: Sophie Grillet

Contents

Foreword

In an economy driven by innovation and constant change, success is dependent on having a flexible organisation. The successful organisation must train its leaders in all the appropriate management skills, and create a culture and structure that allows those skills maximum freedom to take full effect.

Effective teams are necessary for the continual growth, development and day-to-day management of an organisation. Teamwork is the process which allows the organisation to take and implement decisions. The corporate culture within which teams operate will ultimately determine how successful or unsuccessful teams will be.

Senior management philosophy and management style will have a major impact throughout an organisation, and will create either harmony or stress depending on how each manager or supervisor's own style relates to that of the organisation. If managers with a very "open" management style are working within an organisation whose culture is a "closed" management style this can lead to stress for them, although their team can enjoy the benefits of being allowed to share in information and decision making. However, the opposite is also true – combine a "closed" management style with an "open" organisation and it is the team that will suffer and its performance will be affected. Managers therefore need to be sufficiently trained for the process of managing people, understanding cultures, building relationships and ensuring commitment to the organisation.

This book does not set out to be a prescriptive work which will solve any situation. What it does offer is an opportunity to understand the various cultures which organisations have and the different approaches that can be taken by those in supervisory and management positions.

Graham Houston
Head of the Industrial Society
in Scotland and Ireland

Acknowledgements

We would like to thank our colleagues in The Industrial Society for their interest, support and constructive comments, which helped us produce this book.

In particular our thanks must go to Denise Wilson for her patience, word-processing skills, sense of humour and ability to decipher our notes!

 # Introduction

In producing this book our initial thought from a reader's point of view was: what would make it different to the rest of the literature currently available on this subject?

We wanted it to be:

- Practical
- Based on our experience of working with and advising a variety of organisations and developing teambuilding materials for them
- Based on our experience of being team members in different organisations

This publication is not designed to be a "quick fix", and it certainly won't change your life in 10 minutes, but our purpose is to identify and understand the issues and actions of successful teambuilding.

We have created "STOP AND THINK" activities in each chapter to:

- help you take a look at your own team
- identify what steps need to be taken to improve its performance
- enable you to put into practice the appropriate actions that will guide your own team towards more effective working

Leaders are best
When people barely know they exist,
Not so good when people acclaim them,
Worst when they despise them,
But of a good leader, who talks little,
When their work is done, their aim fulfilled,
Their people will all say "We did this
ourselves".

> *from Lao-Tse*
> *(Ancient Chinese*
> *Philosopher)*

1

What is a Team?

"A TEAM IS A GROUP OF PEOPLE WORKING TOWARDS A COMMON OBJECTIVE" (OR IS IT?)

If you were to watch a marathon race you would see a group of individuals working towards a common purpose. They want to run the course to complete it, to meet the challenge. Although they have a common purpose they are not a team.

In this situation they do not need to be one as it would be inappropriate to consider forming a marathon team – it is essentially an individual activity that requires some support and back-up facilities.

Teamwork is perhaps more like running a series of 400m relays with a pause in between to check that the position of the finishing line hasn't changed. Successful relay teams depend on having the strengths of the individuals known to other team members in order to play to those strengths.

Why are so many organisations focusing on the importance of high performance work teams? There is perhaps an age-old balancing act.

QUALITY   **QUANTITY**

The traditional response has been a compromise always between quality and quantity.

- Quantitative in producing output and quantity that can be measured
- Qualitative in terms of how people feel about working for the organisation

In creating high performance teams there is no compromise. Both qualitative and quantitative benefits will occur.

The qualitative aspect should never be underestimated, i.e. creating the environment where people feel they want to give that extra discretionary effort. A strong qualitative culture is never achieved by chance. We believe organisations need to develop at appropriate levels three senses for its employees – a sense of Direction, and a sense of Belonging, a sense of Identity.

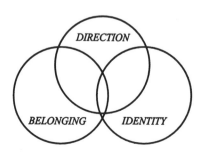

The sense of direction is the vision of the external environment, the strategic intent for the organisation. The sense of direction is very often given in the form of a mission statement. Indeed the use of mission statements is currently an increasing trend across many organisations and sectors.

How effective are mission statements? Are they just pious words or are they genuine statements of organisations?

Mission statements are usually readily available and visible. They may be framed in reception areas, they may be on literature which is handed out to staff and customers alike. Less visible, however, are the foundations, the aspects which underpin the mission statement, just as nine-tenths of the iceberg is below the surface of the water. Mission statements are underpinned by the organisation's values, its cultures. If they are not, then they are worthless.

We have visited organisations that have statements of values on reception walls and then we have observed that they treat people, internally and externally, in ways that bear no relation to these values. Perhaps that is what we mean when we talk about making the mission statement liveable.

The flow chart on page 5 will help you review your organisation's approach to its mission statement, and highlight the five key elements for a successful mission.

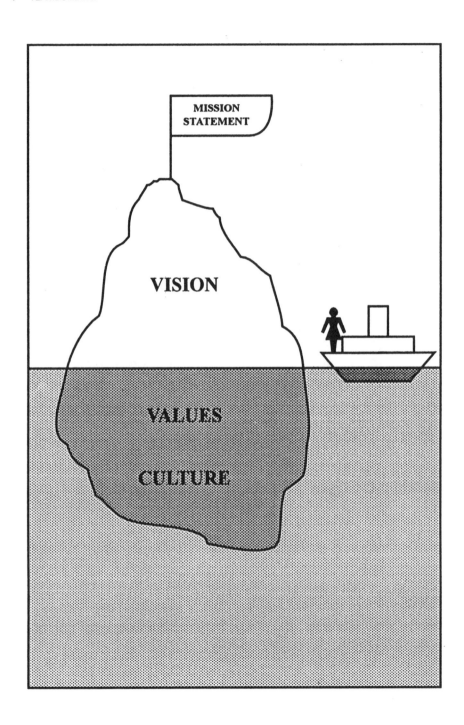

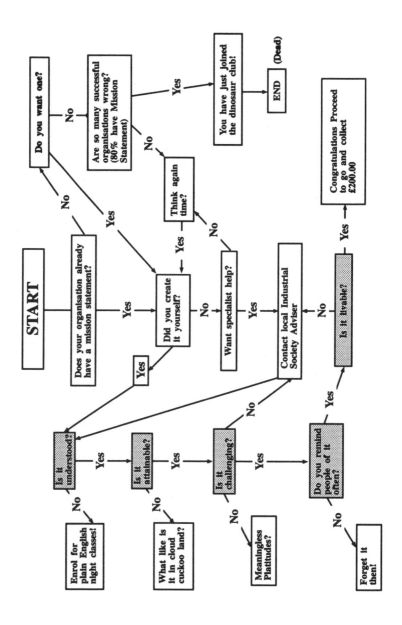

A mission statement should be:

- understandable
- attainable
- challenging
- reinforceable
- liveable

It will not just provide a focus of where the organisation is going but will also be an element of that corporate identity which gives people a sense of belonging to the organisation.

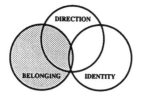

However, it is not enough merely to focus on corporate issues. A **sense of belonging** has to be fostered by every team in the organisation. It will flourish in a high performance team as its members:

- know what needs to be done
- have the confidence in themselves and each other to do it
- will probably enjoy themselves in the process

In this way, a balance is monitored between productivity and the satisfaction of personal team member needs.

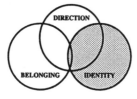

A sense of identity

Individual needs will vary, but a HIGH PERFORMANCE TEAM will create a climate where individuals are valued for themselves and not just for the knowledge and skills that they bring to the team.

The openness, support and trust that is provided by a HIGH PERFORMANCE TEAM will enable people to become aware of their individuality, recognise self-worth and raise self-confidence.

The sense of direction, belonging and identity are **central** to every team.

Whether we are members of a:

- Senior Management Team
- Department Team
- Project Team
- Support Team
- Operator Team

The issues which need to be tackled in building an effective team remain the same.

Stop and Think

Before embarking on any kind of Teambuilding approach we should ask ourselves three questions:

- *Are we a team?*
- *Do we need to be one?*
- *Is our organisation ready and willing to provide the atmosphere, the culture and the support that effective teamworking requires?*

2

Teams and Organisational Cultures

By the end of this chapter you will:

- have analysed the culture of your organisation
- have identified your individual preferred culture
- have understood the relationships between culture and teamwork

The type of cultures exhibited in organisations can stem from two main routes. There is the **corporate** culture, promoted actively by the organisation as the pattern of beliefs which are known, understood and shared by most people in the organisation. Corporate culture is the "keystone" that holds the organisation together as its members share values, beliefs and expectations. It is usually actively promoted by the organisation as vision, mission, strategies and objectives.

The **underpinning** culture is less tangible. It is the willingness of individuals to accept and "buy into" the corporate values and systems. This willingness will be affected by their past experiences and future needs.

The underpinning culture may complement or conflict with the corporate culture.

The following questionnaire was developed by Dr Roger Harrison and is based around his model of different organisational cultures. It has been used extensively as a starting point in looking at this issue. It will highlight the relationship between our individual ideas and values, and the prevailing corporate culture within our organisation.

It will further indicate whether the corporate culture will complement or compete with the concept of teamworking.

We would suggest you work through it all *before* looking at the role-model explanations.

To complete this assessment, start by using the left-hand column and give a rank of "1" to the statement that most accurately represents the dominant or prevailing view in the organisation in your opinion. Assign a "2" to the next most prevalent, and so on through "3" and "4", which represents the view least typically held in the organisation. Complete the left-hand column for all 15 questions.

When you have completed all questions in this way, then (using the right-hand column) indicate which statement reflects most accurately *your own view of the way the organisation should be.* Give this statement a rank of "1" and progress through to the least desired statement which has a rank of "4". (You might wish to conceal the left-hand column when you give your personal view.)

Organisational view	Questions and Statements	Personal view
	1. A good boss is.......	
	a. strong, decisive and firm but fair. Protective, generous and indulgent to loyal employees.	
	b. impersonal and correct, avoiding the exercise of authority for personal advantage. Demands from employees only that which is required by the formal system.	
	c. egalitarian and capable of being influenced in matters about the task. Uses authority to obtain the resources needed to complete the job.	
	d. concerned to be responsive to the personal needs and values of others. Uses position to provide satisfying and growth stimulating work opportunities for employees.	
	2. A good employee is.......	
	a. complementary, hard working and loyal to the interests of the boss.	

Organisational view	Questions and Statements	Personal view
	b. responsive and reliable, meeting the duties and responsibilities of the job and avoiding actions that either surprise or embarrass the boss. c. self-motivated to contribute best performance to the task, and open with ideas and suggestions. Also willing to give the lead to others when they show greater ability or expertise. d. interested in the development of own potential and open to learning and to receiving help. Respects the needs and values of others and is willing to help in their development.	
	3. A good member of the organisation gives priority to the....... a. personal demands of the boss. b. duties, responsibilities and requirements of own role and to the customary standards of personal behaviour. c. requirements of the task for skill, ability, energy and material resources. d. personal needs of the individuals involved.	

Organisational view	Questions and Statements	Personal view
	4. People who do well in this organisation are....... a. shrewd and competitive, with a strong need for power. b. conscientious and responsible, with a strong need for power. c. technically effective and competent, with a strong commitment to getting the job done. d. effective and competent in personal relationships, with a strong commitment to the development and growth of people.	
	5. The organisation treats people as....... a. through their time and energy, at the disposal of people higher up the hierarchy. b. through their time and energy, available through a contract with rights and obligations on both sides. c. colleagues who have committed their skills and abilities to the common cause. d. interesting and worthwhile in their own right.	

Organisational view	Questions and Statements	Personal view
	6. People are controlled and influenced by the....... a. personal exercise of economic and political power (rewards and punishments). b. impersonal exercise of economic and personal power to enforce procedures or standards of performance. c. communication and discussion of task requirements leading to appropriate action motivated by personal commitment. d. intrinsic interest and enjoyment to be found in their activities and/or by concern and caring for the needs of the others.	
	7. It is legitimate for one person to control another's activities if....... a. the person has more power and authority in the organisation. b. the role prescribes that the person son holds authority to direct others. c. the person has more knowledge relevant to the job than another? d. the other accepts that the first person's help can contribute to personal learning and growth in the job?	

Organisational view	Questions and Statements	Personal view
	8. The basis of task allocations is the...	
	a. personal judgement and needs of those in authority.	
	b. formal divisions of functions and responsibilities in the system.	
	c. resource and expertise requirements of the job to be done.	
	d. personal wishes and need for learning and development of individual organisation members.	
	9. Work is done out of.......	
	a. hope of reward, fear of punishment or personal loyalty to a powerful individual.	
	b. respect for the obligations of the contract, backed up by sanctions and loyalty to the organisation of the system.	
	c. satisfaction in work excellence and achievement, and/or personal commitment to the task or goal.	
	d. enjoyment of the activity for its own sake, and concern and respect for the needs and values of work colleagues involved.	

Organisational view	Questions and Statements	Personal view
	10. People work together when.......	
	a. they are required to do so by higher authority, or when they believe they can use each other for personal advantage.	
	b. co-ordination and exchange are specified by the formal system.	
	c. their joint contribution is needed to perform the task.	
	d. the collaboration is personally rewarding, stimulating or challenging.	
	11. The purpose of the competition is to.......	
	a. gain personal power and advantage.	
	b. gain high status positions in the formal system.	
	c. increase the excellence of contributions to the task at hand.	
	d. draw attention to one's own personal needs and skills.	

Organisational view	Questions and Statements	Personal view
	12. Conflict is....... a. controlled by the intervention of higher authorities and often fostered by them to enhance or maintain their own power. b. suppressed by reference to rules, regulations or procedures and the definitions of authority and responsibility. c. resolved through full discussion of the merits of the work issues involved. d. resolved by open and deep discussion of the values and ethics of the people involved.	
	13. Decisions are made by the....... a. person with the highest power and authority. b. person whose job description carries and defines the responsibility. c. people with the most expertise and knowledge of the problem. d. people most personally involved and affected by the outcome.	

Organisational view	Questions and Statements	Personal view
	14. In appropriate control & communication structures......	
	a. command flows from the top down in a simple pyramid, in which anyone higher has authority over anyone who is lower. Information flows up the chain.	
	b. directives flow from top down and information flows upwards in functional pyramids which meet at the top. Authority and responsibility flows down and is limited to its own pyramid. Cross-functional exchange is limited or difficult.	
	c. information about task problems and requirements flows down from the activity upwards and outwards. Those closest to the task determine the resources and support needed from the organisation. There are co-ordination structures to link related task centres, and these shift as the focus of the tasks shift.	
	d. information and influence flow between people based on relationships initiated for the purpose of work, learning, shared values or enjoyment. A co-ordinating function may establish overall levels of contribution needed for the organisation to survive, and tasks are assigned by mutual agreement.	

Organisational view	Questions and Statements	Personal view
	15. The environment is responded to as though it were.....	
	a. a competitive jungle in which everyone is against everyone else, and those who do not exploit others are themselves exploited.	
	b. an orderly and rational system in which competition is limited by rules, and there can be negotiation and machinery to resolve conflicts.	
	c. a complex of imperfect forms and systems which are reshaped and improved in response to organisational achievements.	
	d. a complex of potential threat and support used by the organisation both as a means of self-nourishment and as a play.	

SCORESHEET

Sum the scores for "a's", "b's", "c's" and "d's" from the left-hand column of the questionnaire to get Existing Organisational Climate scores. Similarly sum from the right-hand column to get your own Preferred Organisational Climate. Low scores indicate predominant ideology, high scores the less seen (or wanted) ideology. Enter your scores in the appropriate boxes below.

Existing Organisational Climate		Your Preferred Climate
	a POWER ORIENTATION	
	b ROLE ORIENTATION	
	c TASK ORIENTATION	
	d PEOPLE ORIENTATION	

What then do these orientations mean?

Charles Handy in his book *Gods of Management* further develops Harrison's model, and relates to each orientation the attributes of a particular Greek god.

He suggests the following:

1 POWER CULTURE

The structure of power culture can best be illustrated as a spider's web.

If this culture had a patron god it would be Zeus, the all-powerful God of Ancient Greece who ruled by whim and impulse, by thunderbolt and shower of gold from Mount Olympus.

This culture depends on a central power source, with rays of power and influence spreading out from that central figure. The rays are connected by functional or specialist

strings, but the power rings are the centres of activity and influence.

The organisation depends on trust and empathy for its effectiveness and on telepathy and personal conversation for communication. If the centre chooses the right people, who can think in the same way as it thinks, they can be left to get on with the job. There are few rules and procedures and little bureaucracy. Control is exercised by the centre, largely through the selection of key individuals by occasional forays from the centre or summonses to the centre.

Organisations that exhibit these characteristics may include:

Smallish entrepreneurial organisations, some property finance and trading companies. Situations where the key figure has often created and grown up with the organisation and may have difficulty in delegating or creating new structures as the size of the organisation grows.

What might other limiting factors of this culture be?

- size
- retention of key individuals
- the "spider" dies or retires

Size is a problem for power cultures. The web can break if it seeks to link too many activities; indeed the only way the web organisation can grow and remain a web is by spawning other organisations, other spiders.

These cultures put a lot of faith in the individual, little in committees. They judge by results and are tolerant of means. They are often seen as tough or abrasive. Though successful they may well suffer from low morale and high staff turnover in the middle layers as individuals fail or opt out of the competitive atmosphere. And it must be remembered that these cultures may run out of power. Many of the family businesses that stagnated in Britain after the Second World War were power cultures that had died in the centre. A web without a spider has no strength.

> We recognised the spider in a Chief Executive of a group of companies who had worked his way to the top over the course of his working life. He had started with the company at the age of 16, was a self-made man and was justly proud of his achievements. He had, however, definite spider tendencies. Every night, half an hour after close of business, managers could guarantee a phone call just asking how things had gone that day. Woe betide any manager not remaining behind and completing the voluntary (unpaid) over-time expected by his boss.

2 ROLE CULTURE

This structure can best be illustrated as a Greek temple.

Its patron god is Apollo, the god of reason, for this culture works by logic and rationality. The Role Organisation rests its strength in its pillars, its functions or specialities. These pillars are strong in their own right; the finance department, the purchasing department, the production facility may be internationally renowned for their efficiency. The work of the pillars, and the interaction between the pillars, is controlled by:

- Procedures for roles, e.g. job descriptions, authority definitions
- Procedures for communications, e.g. appeal to the lowest crossover points

They are co-ordinated at the top by a narrow band of senior management, the pediment. It is assumed that this should be the only personal co-ordination needed, for as the separate pillars do their job, as laid down by the rules and procedures, the ultimate result will be as planned.

In this culture the role, or job description, is often more important than the individual who fills it.

Individuals are selected for satisfactory performance of a role, and the role is usually so described that a range of individuals could fill it. Performance over and above the role prescription is not required, and indeed can be disruptive at times.

Organisations that may exhibit these include:
Large or bureaucratic organisations operating in a stable environment where there is little sudden change to affect them. They often operate in monopoly-type situations, where quick decision making is not required.

The limiting factors in a Role Culture are:

- departmentalisation, leading to lack of common vision
- inability to make decisions without referring them upwards

The more management layers that are in place (itself an indicator of severe "departmentalising" philosophy) the more difficult it becomes to get a decision at operating levels. A decision needs to go through so many layers that it will either be lost, side-tracked, or filtered; or just too late. Departmentalisation leads to compartmentalism.

In some of the "role"-type organisations we have encountered, the position of individuals within the hierarchy is characterised by the allocation of china cups, whether they are allowed chocolate biscuits for visitors and what specific type of carpets and furnishings they are allowed in their office.

It has been known in some of these organisations that, following restructuring, the curtains and carpets were removed from the offices of people whose grades no longer merit them.

3 TASK CULTURE

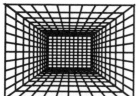 Here the emphasis is also on getting the job done, but by forming groups or teams in order to do it. It can be linked to a matrix.

Its patron goddess is Athena, the goddess of knowledge and wisdom. Athenian cultures tend to think of individuals as resourceful humans rather than human resources.

Influence within this culture is based on expertise and ability to get the job done, rather than position within the organisation or personal power. The Task Culture can be highly adaptable – groups, project teams, or task forces are formed for a specific purpose and can be reformed, abandoned or continued.

Specific issues are focused on, but sometimes common vision of the organisation's objectives can be overlooked.

"They can't see the wood for the trees."

Other limiting factors include:

- co-ordination of other groups outside the team's normal operating arena
- availability of individuals
- ability of individuals available

We recently visited an organisation that had adapted a Task Culture from its previous position of a power/role combination. The Managing Director was very concerned that "the new structure wasn't working out as planned".

Three factors had not been planned well enough:

1   Individuals require time to adjust to a situational, empowering culture to establish what exactly they can do (and that no-one is telling them they can't).

2   Possible casualties (ex-managers) uncomfortable with their lack of "status" in the new structure and who will consciously or sub-consciously undermine it.

3   Within the flattened structure there had been redundancies among some middle managers. The way in which the redundancies had been carried out had sent shock waves throughout the organisation.
"Betty's years of experience didn't count for anything."

It will take time and nurturing to regain the confidence and commitment of the remaining staff who believe that in its desire to achieve the new structure, the organisation had dispensed with a valuable source of knowledge and experience.

How much better it might have proved to involve Betty in an adjustment period by, perhaps, offering her a part-time consultancy role to help achieve the new structure, and provide an umbilical cord while she found a new position. How much better for the organisation, for the remaining employees, and for Betty's self-respect and perception of her own value.

4   A more unusual culture is the **PEOPLE CULTURE** which

resembles a cell under the microscope and is represented by Dionysus, the God of Wine and Song. The culture where the individual is paramount.

If the culture has any structure it is flexible, existing only to serve the individuals within it.

Typical People Cultures may be architects' partnerships, legal practices, small consultancies, co-operative ventures within individual trades, e.g. open air markets.

Identifying factors are considerable personal freedom and autonomy, a high degree of flexibility, and in some cases a lack of formal policies and procedures: "I'll get the job done and worry about the rules (if they exist) later."

Limiting factors include:

- lack of overall strategy
- size
- individual talents

A successful and sustained example of a people culture is the Findhorn community in Scotland.

Founded in the sixties as a co-operative of craftspeople, sharing the same resources, but with the autonomy to develop and market their own products, the community exists to serve the interests of its people.

We have administered this culture questionnaire to a large number of individuals, from different sectors, locations and management levels, during the course of our work.

We have discovered two main factors:

- There tends to be an almost equal split between organisations perceived to be operating in Power/Role/Task modes. (People cultures are much less common, i.e. 3–4% only.)
- 94% of respondents select the Task Culture as their own preferred operating climate.

We have one final thought on cultural awareness at this stage.

The Industrial Society recently carried out a major survey of its members to identify what were seen as key issues by middle and senior managers in sending first line managers on a training course – in particular, what subjects did they wish to be included in the courses?

In carrying out this survey we also amassed details of the titles organisations allocated to their first line managers – e.g. supervisor, foreperson, chargehand, section leader.

In the table, we provide a summary of subjects requested and title of the job holder.

FOREMAN/WOMAN	%	*TEAM LEADER*	%
1 Health and safety	62	1 Teambuilding	70
2 Motivation	52	2 Interpersonal skills	62
3 Maintaining discipline	50	3 Motivation	60
4 Decision taking	48	4 Delegation	55
5 Interpersonal skills	45	5 Health and safety	55

Maintaining discipline was ranked 23rd and attributed 19% by organisations with team leaders. *Teambuilding* was ranked 8th and attributed 40% by organisations with forepersons

- The traditional management approach appears to be

  – control
  – supervision
  – enforcement
  – its my job to motivate you

- The team approach requires

  – guiding
  – enabling
  – creating a climate for people to fulfil their own levels of motivation and decision making

Stop and Think

Before you commit to teamworking:

- *Which approach is prevalent in your organisation?*
- *Are there changes that need to be made?*
- *What are they?*
- *How can you make them?*

3

Team Composition

In this chapter we will:

- discover the difference between team role and team functions
- examine new teams – project teams – inherited/existing teams
- learn of the balance that should be present within a high performance team
- see how organisations can use indicators to help individuals to discover their preferred roles through indicators
- discuss the rising trend of using psychometric assessments in recruitment and team selection processes

New Teams

Imagine you are in a park one weekend when you are approached by a friend and asked if you could help make up one side in a local charity hockey tournament the following week.

Your friend knows you are reasonably fit and have good eye/hand/ball co-ordination because you play golf and tennis together quite regularly.

You have never played hockey before in your life

You are given two small books entitled *The Rules of Hockey*, and a *Brief History of the Game*, and requested to read them before next Saturday.

Your friend also gives you a written narrative analysing a famous player in action and comments "you might get some idea of what to do from this description."

The following Saturday your apprehension increases when you arrive at the pitch and discover another 10 players in the same predicament as yourself!

You are effectively, a new team, in a new environment, together only in as much as you are athletic enough to run with, and hit a ball individually for the duration of the match.

You are a member of a group selected for technical skills or function with no consideration given to personality traits and interaction between the individuals.

There are 40 minutes prior to the tournament commencing and you decide to have a warm-up and try and sort out the team. At this stage you discover that some players prefer to be attackers, some defenders, and you personally feel most comfortable in goal. The team has started to discover team roles – that different approaches may feel more natural to different players, and in this case there is the scope and freedom for them to follow these natural preferences. But of course this was after all a hypothetical example – how often does it happen in real life?

Project Teams

There are two observations that have been made from advisory and training work carried out by The Industrial Society specifically in team working:

- Increasing numbers of organisations are developing flatter structures and moving towards project teams working within a matrix-style task function.
- 94% of respondents in identifying their preferred operating climate (see page 28) will select the task culture. (Look back at your choice – if you are in the 6% can you identify why this is the case?)

It would appear that, if handled well a considerable motivational opportunity exists for many people in many organisations to:

- create a structure with which they can identify
- enable them to develop in a project team
- combine technical expertise with an awareness of their preferred role, ie attacker/defender/goal keeper
- provide an environment to celebrate team success

Project Teams have, by implied definition, a finite time in which to be in existence – ie the duration of the project. For some longer-term projects, this may involve members leaving and others replacing them. In these situations it becomes vital that team role as well as team functions are combined, so that the balance and harmony within the remainder of the team are not disturbed.

Existing/Inherited Teams

For many people there may not be the comparative luxury of selecting a team from scratch. You have to manage with an existing group of individuals – without, in most cases, the escape of a project conclusion to enable you to re-group or re-form.

This is the reality and the challenge of building an effective team. What happens if you have inherited a team composed entirely of attackers? Or if everyone would prefer to be in goal? How do you build a winning team if everyone is pre-occupied with defending their positions?

The first step is to encourage team role awareness, and to analyse the composition of your existing team.

Team Role Indicators

There are currently a wealth of systems available to organi-sations, indicators which may be used to illustrate team members' preferred role(s).

Sometimes there may be no clear single preference – that person being equally comfortable in two or more roles. In some cases a member may record a zero score in certain categories – it should not be assumed that this person *cannot* undertake this role, just that it may not feel comfortable to them and if a choice exists they would normally avoid this type of behaviour.

Different indicators may have identified a varying number of team roles and given them different names – For example:

The Strength Deployment Inventory†

identifies 4 roles and a blend of another 3, using colours as a convenient identifying system, within the framework of a triangle.

Magerison & McCann‡

base their roles around a wheel and have identified 8 choices.

Glen Parker in his book *Team Players and Team Work* talks about four roles. He has named them the Contributor, Collaborator, Communicator and Challenger.

Perhaps the most well known, used, and documented indicator in this country is based on the work carried out by Dr Meredith Belbin at the Administrative Staff College at Henley.

Belbin used as a source of data a business game with eight teams competing against each other, this game being one part of a 10-week management development programme. Over a period of seven years he and his researchers amassed large amounts of data on team composition and respective performance, and achieved an impressive record in predicting team performance. Belbin acknowledges that it is far easier to forecast teams that will fail, than teams sure to succeed. In this respect there is a pre-disposition with most managers to pick a team composed of the cleverest and most talented people they could find. Unfortunately for them, Belbin discovered that the most disaster-prone team is the one exclusively composed of very clever people.

† copyright Elias H. Porter and Sara E. Maloney
‡ copyright Magerison & McCann

Dr Belbin and his colleagues learned also to recognise individuals who could make a crucial difference to team performance, and he named those eight types. The reason for these names may not always be obvious, but it seems sensible to use them, with the disclaimer that it is the descriptions, not the labels that are important.

Not everyone tested by Belbin belonged clearly to one of the eight types – about 30% showed no real preferences.

Reproduced below is the questionnaire to identify self team role preferences. We suggest you complete it now before you read the accompanying team role descriptions.

To complete each section of this Inventory, tick in the far left-hand column the one, two or three sentences most applicable to yourself.

Then in the column on the right, apportion 10 points between those sentences you have ticked, thus indicating the relative extent to which each applies.

For example, in one section you might feel there are only two sentences that apply to you: one of which you feel sums you up well while the other only applies some of the time. In this instance you could give your first choice seven points and the remaining points to your second choice. In some instances you might decide that there are two sentences which apply to you equally – if this is the case, award five points to each.

You must allocate all 10 points in each section

The Belbin Questionnaire

SECTION A

WHEN INVOLVED IN A PROJECT WITH OTHER PEOPLE:

TICK   POINTS

1. I can be relied upon to see that work that needs to be done is organised.
2. I pick up slips and omissions that others fail to notice.
3. I react strongly when meetings look like losing track of the main objective.
4. I produce original suggestions.
5. I analyse other people's ideas objectively, for both merits and failings.
6. I am keen to find out the latest ideas and developments.
7. I have an aptitude for organising people.
8. I am always ready to support good suggestions that help to resolve a problem.

SECTION B

IN SEEKING SATISFACTION THROUGH MY WORK:

TICK   POINTS

	1. I like to have a strong influence on decisions.	
	2. I feel in my element where work requires a high degree of attention and concentration.	
	3. I am concerned to help colleagues with their problems.	
	4. I like to make critical discrimination between alternatives.	
	5. I tend to have a creative approach to problem solving.	
	6. I enjoy reconciling different points of view.	
	7. I am more interested in practicalities than in new ideas.	
	8. I particularly enjoy exploring different views and techniques.	

SECTION C

WHEN THE TEAM IS TRYING TO SOLVE A PARTICULARLY COMPLEX PROBLEM:

TICK   POINTS

	1. I keep a watching eye on areas where difficulty may arise.	
	2. I explore ideas that may have a wider application than in the immediate task.	
	3. I like to weigh up and evaluate a range of suggestions thoroughly before choosing.	
	4. I can co-ordinate and use productively other people's abilities and talents.	
	5. I maintain a steady systematic approach, whatever the pressures.	
	6. I often produce a new approach to a long continuing problem.	
	7. I am ready to make my personal views known in a forceful way if necessary.	
	8. I am ready to help whenever I can.	

SECTION D

IN CARRYING OUT MY DAY-TO-DAY WORK:

TICK   POINTS

	1. I am keen to see there is nothing vague about my task and objectives.	
	2. I am not reluctant to emphasise my own point of view in meetings.	
	3. I can work with all sorts of people provided that they have got something worthwhile to contribute.	
	4. I make a point of following up interesting ideas and/or people.	
	5. I can usually find the argument to refute unsound propositions.	
	6. I tend to see patterns where others would see items as unconnected.	
	7. Being busy gives me real satisfaction.	
	8. I have a quiet interest in getting to know people better.	

SECTION E

IF I AM SUDDENLY GIVEN A DIFFICULT TASK WITH LIMITED TIME AND UNFAMILIAR PEOPLE:

TICK   POINTS

	1. I often find my imagination frustrated by working in a group.	
	2. I find my personal skill particularly appropriate in achieving agreement.	
	3. My feelings seldom interfere with my judgement.	
	4. I strive to build up an effective structure.	
	5. I can work with people who vary widely in their personal qualities and outlook.	
	6. I feel it is sometimes worth incurring some temporary unpopularity if one is to succeed in getting one's views across in a group.	
	7. I usually know someone whose specialist knowledge is particularly apt.	
	8. I seem to develop a natural sense of urgency.	

SECTION F

WHEN SUDDENLY ASKED TO CONSIDER A NEW PROJECT:

TICK   POINTS

1. I start to look around for possible ideas and openings.	
2. I am concerned to finish and perfect current work before I start.	
3. I approach the problem in a carefully analytical way.	
4. I am able to assert myself to get other people involved if necessary.	
5. I am able to take an independent and innovative look at most situations.	
6. I am happy to take the lead when action is required.	
7. I can respond positively to my colleagues and their initiatives.	
8. I find it hard to give in a job where the goals are not clearly defined.	

SECTION G

IN CONTRIBUTING TO GROUP PROJECTS IN GENERAL:

TICK		POINTS
	1. I think I have a talent for sorting out the concrete steps that need to be taken given a broad brief.	
	2. My considered judgement may take time but is usually near the mark.	
	3. A broad range of personal contacts is important to my style of working.	
	4. I have an eye for getting the details right.	
	5. I try to make my mark in group meetings.	
	6. I can see how ideas and techniques can be used in new relationships.	
	7. I see both sides of a problem and take a decision acceptable to all.	
	8. I get on well with others and work hard for the team.	

SCORING KEY FOR PERSONAL INVENTORY

Transfer your points allocation from the seven sections of
the Personal Inventory to the appropriate boxes below.
The pre-printed numbers in the grid refer to the question
numbers of each section. For example if for Section A you
scored seven points for question 6 and three points for
question 1 you would allocate them in the columns headed
RI and IMP respectively.

	SH	CO	PL	RI	ME	IMP	TW	F
A	3_	7_	4_	6_	5_	1_	8_	2_
B	1_	6_	5_	8_	4_	7_	3_	2_
C	7_	4_	6_	2_	3_	5_	8_	1_
D	2_	3_	6_	4_	5_	1_	8_	7_
E	6_	5_	1_	7_	3_	4_	2_	8_
F	6_	4_	5_	1_	3_	8_	7_	2_
G	5_	7_	6_	3_	2_	1_	8_	4_
TOTAL								

Once you have allocated all your points, total each column.

The highest two totals represent your primary and sec-
ondary preferred team roles.

The eight individual types identified by Belbin are:

- Chairperson/Co-ordinator (CO)
- Shaper (SH)
- Plant (PL)
- Resource/Investigator (RI)
- Monitor/Evaluator (ME)
- Company Worker/Implementer (IMP)
- Team Worker (TW)
- Finisher (F)

These are described on the following pages.

The Belbin questionnaire reproduced with kind permission by the publishers from *Management Teams – Why They Succeed or Fail* (Butter-worth-Heinemann).

CHAIRPERSON/CO-ORDINATOR (CO)

- Co-ordinates the way the team moves towards group objectives
- Makes best use of team resources
- Recognises team strengths and weaknesses
- Maximises the potential of each team member

Positive qualities

- Welcomes all contributions on their merit
- Strong sense of objectives

Allowable weaknesses

- Is unlikely to be the most creative member of the team

SHAPER (SH)

- Shapes the way in which team effort is channelled
- Directs attention to the setting of objectives and priorities
- Seeks to impose a shape or pattern on group discussions and outcomes

Positive qualities

- Drive and a readiness to challenge inertia, ineffectiveness, complacency and self-deception

Allowable weaknesses

- Prone to provocation, irritation and impatience

PLANT (PL)

- Advances new ideas and strategies
- Pays special attention to major issues
- Creative approach to problem-solving

Positive qualities

- Imagination, intellect, knowledge

Allowable weaknesses

- Inclined to disregard practical details or protocol

RESOURCE/INVESTIGATOR (RI)

- Explores and reports on ideas and developments outside the team
- Creates external contacts

Positive qualities

- Capacity for contacting people and exploring anything new
- Ability to respond to challenge

Allowable weaknesses

- Loses interest once the initial fascination has passed.

MONITOR/EVALUATOR (ME)

- Analyses problems, evaluates ideas and suggestions
- Enables team to take balanced decisions

Positive qualities

- Judgement, discretion, hard-headedness

Allowable weaknesses

- May lack inspiration and ability to motivate others

COMPANY WORKER/IMPLEMENTER (IMP)

- Turns concepts and plans into practical working procedures
- Carries out agreed plans systematically and efficiently

Positive qualities

- Organising ability, practical common sense
- Self-disciplined, hard-working

Allowable weaknesses

- Lack of flexibility, unresponsive to new or unproven ideas

TEAM WORKER (TW)

- Supports team members in their strengths
- Builds on suggestions
- Compensates for team members' shortcomings
- Improves communication between members

Positive qualities

- Ability to respond to people and situations
- Promotes team spirit

Allowable weaknesses

- May be indecisive at moments of crisis

FINISHER (F)

- Ensures nothing has been overlooked
- Checks details
- Maintains a sense of urgency

Positive qualities

- Capacity for follow-through
- Perfectionism

Allowable weaknesses

- Tendency to worry about small things
- Reluctant to let go

So how might Belbin be used within an existing team?

- It is a relatively low risk activity for a team as it highlights strengths and "allowable weaknesses". Thus there are no winners or losers in the analysis.

- Human nature being what it is, there is an inherent curiosity to "see how I come out and how others score in my team".

- It provides a most valuable insight on others' self-perceptions and usually provokes a great deal of discussion – "Yes you did that last week when you . . ." or "That's interesting – I don't see you in that way usually".

- It allows the existing team to modify its behaviour in order to compensate for any obvious omissions in team role make-up. For example a team with no finisher might constantly have had problems in the past in meeting specific deadlines.

With Belbin awareness a team member with a higher finisher score than his/her colleagues might then recognise that the rest of the team require that member to concentrate more on progress-chasing and keeping them to time.

Indeed for a team with no obvious finisher, another approach might be to appoint one formally for each project or task – in essence giving that member implied authority to chase the rest of the team for results, without any offence being taken.

Stop and Think

There can be three drawbacks to team role indicators:

- *Having them all does not automatically guarantee success (not having them all, and taking no remedial action, does however increase the likelihood of failure)*
- *They are usually based on self perception inventories or questionnaires and can therefore be subjective*
- *There can be dangers of stereotyping and putting people into permanent boxes ("Why do you expect Chris is a Shaper?") etc.*

Many organisations use other forms of assessment in addition to Team Role Indicators. These methods may, in many cases, involve occupational psychologists and more than one method of assessment in order to increase the confidence factor of accurate findings. Collective assessments are commonly known as a battery, and below we have detailed a very brief description of some of the most commonly used methods of psychometric assessment.

Cattell's 16 PF

The 16 Personality Factor questionnaire was developed over 40 years ago in the US, initially for research and clinical purposes. However, for many years it has been used for general personality assessment and an enormous amount of research into its technical properties and its applications has been carried out. Detailed results are published in the 16 PF Handbook. There are four forms for general use, each with British norms: Forms A and B, which are full versions, and C and D which are shorter versions, with simpler language for those with low educational attainment. All forms measure the same 16 primary factors and four second-order factors: introversion-extroversion; emotional stability; tough-poise; and independence.

The questionnaire is used for both occupational assessment and counselling. All versions are untimed and take between 25 and 60 minutes to complete.

Saville and Holdsworth's (SHL) Occupational Personality Questionnaire (OPQ)

The OPQ was published in 1984 after four years of systematic development in the UK. It is designed specifically to assess personality characteristics in the world of work for assessment and counselling purposes. There are 15 different versions, with various response formats used in each version. Therefore some are more suitable for selection purposes, others for counselling. The main domain of personality measured by the OPQ are: relationships with people; thinking style; and feelings and emotions. The longest form, Concept Model, assesses 30 primary factors and takes about 60 minutes to complete, whilst the shortest, Pentagon, measures five dimensions and takes about 10 minutes. The manual contains British norms for all versions. Managerial and professional and graduate norms are available for different versions. Extensive reliability data on all versions are presented. Supplements to the manual, covering additional norms and research data are produced on a regular basis. A detailed report of numerous validation study results is available. Some versions have been translated into a number of different European languages as well as Japanese.

Myers-Briggs Type Indicator

This American personality questionnaire has been developed over the last 40 years and is based on Jung's theory of types. It contains four scales: introversion-extroversion; sensing-intuition; thinking-feeling; and judging-perceptive. Scores can be reported as continuous variables or as a specific type code. There are two versions, Form J and a shorter Form G, which are both untimed and usually take around 60 and 30 minutes respectively to complete. The Indicator is used primarily in personal counselling, although there is also limited evidence of its value as a selection aid. The manual contains American norms for interpretation.

4 Team Development

After reading this chapter you will:

- be aware of the stages of development of a team
- be able to relate those stages to effective team leadership
- be able to understand the way in which the development of the team can positively affect the results that can be achieved within an organisation
- be able to identify priority issues within your own team

The research that has been carried out in the area of Team Development, as well as the experience of teams in a wide variety of organisations, shows that teams have a dynamic of their own. They grow and develop and in doing so they go through several different stages – each with its own distinctive characteristics.

You can assess what stage your team is at through using some different models. One of the best known and most helpful models is Tuckmans:

TUCKMAN'S MODEL:

- Forming
- Storming
- Norming
- Performing

MOVING THROUGH THE FOUR STAGES OF TEAM DEVELOPMENT

1. FORMING

Recognisable features of the forming stage are:

- At work we are nearly always appointed to take over existing/established teams
- We rarely have the chance to select and build our own teams
- The initial adjustment period is often a painful process of misunderstanding
- Leaders try to stamp their authority whilst teams assess them
- Acceptance or rejection of the leaders depends on whether the team will accept (and therefore follow) them
- Many leaders try to bolster their ego by status symbols
- Winning the respect of members takes time and effort

Development actions

- Get to know and assess one another
- Examine the function and purpose of the team
- Look at the skills, knowledge, cohesiveness and balance already present
- Identify the blocks, frustrations and culture

Possible pitfalls

- It is vital to avoid the common mistake of jumping to conclusions too quickly and imposing "instant" changes

- Human chemistry is also an important factor – people can sometimes react and affect each other very negatively and destructively
- If you are selecting new members it is essential to do this job properly. The newcomer should be able to "fit in" with the existing team and add to it
- Flexible structuring is required in the forming stage to allow people to be tested and changed around

2. STORMING

Recognisable features of the storming stage are:
- Feelings begin to come out into the open
- Team is focused on inner conflicts
- Team copes poorly when real pressure comes
- "Peacemakers" paper over cracks and make everything appear "cosy" on the surface
- Team may have an unrealistic view of its own effectiveness

Development actions
- Debate risky issues
- Consider wider options
- Encourage openness and feedback
- Handle conflict positively

Possible pitfalls
- It takes time to build trust
- This stage cannot be rushed
- Some teams are unable to move out of this stage without external help

3. NORMING

Recognisable features of the norming stage are:
- Groundrules are established
- Working procedures are agreed

- High level of concern for a methodical approach to the task
- Closer working relations based on mutual trust and respect
- An ability to discuss and deal with problems and conflicts in an objective way

Development actions

- Maintain openness
- Regular team review
- Encourage challenges to established ways of doing things
- Celebrate success
- Focus on individual as well as team development

Possible pitfalls

- Established methods become an end in themselves
- Creativity is stifled
- Team forgets to look outwards

4. PERFORMING

Recognisable features of the performing stage are:

- High flexibility
- Commitment to team goals
- Problem solving approach
- Conflicting views are handled positively and constructively. Issues are resolved by consensus not majority rule
- Participative leadership
- Group synergy is achieved $2 + 2 = 5$

Teams are never static; once the performing stage has been reached it is vital to keep the team process under regular review to ensure that you stay there.

Another description of the development of a team towards a state of maturity is the model formulated by W. R. Bion.

Bion put forward the idea that not only do teams go through stages of development but this also affects team behaviour so that members behave "as if" they hold onto certain basic assumptions. He also identified four stages:

- **Dependency:** where the team behaves "as if" its members were incapable of making decisions for themselves or of taking care of themselves, so they look for strong directive leadership and expect the leader always to be the person who takes the initiative.
- **Fight/flight:** where the team behaves "as if" it is under threat internally or externally. It begins to recognise other problems than that of authority, however it is not ready to deal with them. It is at this stage that the team may draw together and overreact to a perceived threat from another team or department, or alternatively in-fighting can occur.
- **Pairings:** where individuals begin to offer support to one another in pairs or sub-groups: the team will then behave "as if" the impact of the pairings or sub-groups is highly influential on the life of the team.
- **Maturity:** Team is fully developed. It and can produce effective work and can deal with its emotional problems without threatening its stability.

No model can of itself adequately reflect the complexity of the dynamics of any particular team. However models do provide an opportunity to reflect on and understand a little more clearly where a team is. These models should provide a starting point to think about what needs to be done to move your team through the stages of development to the mature performing stage.

Clearly, then, the leadership style that is appropriate for

a team in an early stage of its development will not be appropriate, or indeed effective, for a team in a later stage.

Tuckmans vs.	*Hershey and Blanchard*
(Team Stages)	(Leader's Style)
Forming	Tell
Storming	Sell
Norming	Participate
Performing	Delegate

An effective team is one which is self-conscious about its own operations. It should regularly review itself, not only in terms of the job to be done but also in terms of its group process. This can provide a valuable opportunity for team leaders to assess the appropriateness of their leadership style.

Team Reviews should take into account the following elements (based on *Building Blocks of Effective Teams* by Mike Woodcock).

- Roles
- Objectives
- Openness and confrontation
- Support and trust
- Co-operation and conflict
- Procedures
- Appropriate leadership
- Review
- Development of individuals
- Good relationship with other groups
- Good communications

An ability to enable the team to assess itself on a regular basis using these issues as guidelines is as important to the health of the team as regular medical checks are to the health of the individual.

Understanding the way in which teams develop, helping your team to move through the stages, and carrying out a process of regular review can make a significant impact on the effectiveness of your team.

Glen Parker's *Team Players and Teamwork* identifies the following features in a team at the "performing" level:

ATMOSPHERE

The "atmosphere" which can be sensed in a few minutes of observation is usually informal, comfortable and relaxed. There are no obvious tensions. It is a working atmosphere in which people are involved and interested. There are no signs of boredom.

DISCUSSION CONTENT

There is a lot of discussion in which virtually everyone participates, but it remains pertinent to the task of the group. If the discussion strays from the subject, someone will quickly bring it back into line.

GROUP OBJECTIVES

The task or the objective of the group is well understood and accepted by the members. There will have been free discussion of the objective at some point until it was formulated in such a way that the members of the group could commit themselves to it.

COMMUNICATIONS

The members listen to each other! The discussion does not have the quality of jumping from one idea to another unrelated one. Every idea is given a hearing. People do not appear to be afraid of being foolish by putting forth a creative thought even if it seems fairly extreme.

HANDLING CONFLICT

There is disagreement. The group is comfortable with this and shows no signs of having to avoid conflict or to keep everything on a plane of sweetness and light. Disagreements are not suppressed or overridden by premature group action. The reasons are carefully examined, and the group seeks to resolve them rather than to dominate the dissenter.

On the other hand, there is no "tyranny of the minority". Individuals who disagree do not appear to be trying to dominate the group or to express hostility. Their disagreement is an expression of a genuine difference of opinion, and they expect a hearing in order that a solution may be found.

Sometimes there are basic disagreements which cannot be resolved. The group finds it impossible to live with them, accepting them but not permitting them to block its efforts. Under some conditions, action will be deferred to permit further study of an issue between the members. On other occasions where the disagreement cannot be resolved and action is necessary, it will be taken but with open caution and recognition that the action may be subject to reconsideration.

DECISION MAKING

Most decisions are reached by a kind of consensus in which it is clear that everybody is in general agreement and willing to go along. However, there is little tendency for individuals who oppose the action to keep their opposition private and thus let an apparent consensus mask real disagreement. Formal voting is at a minimum; the group does not accept a simple majority as a proper basis for action.

CRITICISM

Criticism is frequent, frank and relatively comfortable. There is little evidence of personal attack, either openly or in a hidden fashion. The criticism has a constructive flavour in that it is orientated toward removing an obstacle that faces the group and prevents it from getting the job done.

EXPRESSION OF PERSONAL FEELINGS

People are free in expressing their feelings as well as their ideas both on the problem and on the group's operation. There is little pussyfooting, there are few "hidden agendas". Everybody appears to know quite well how everybody else feels about any matter under discussion.

TASK ACHIEVEMENT

When action is taken, clear assignments are made and accepted.

LEADERSHIP

Group leaders do not dominate a group, nor, on the contrary, does the group defer unduly to them. In fact, as one observes the activity, it is clear that the leadership shifts from time to time, depending on the circumstances.

Different members, because of their knowledge or experience, are in a position at various times to act as "resources" for the group. The members utilise them in this fashion and they occupy leadership roles while they are thus being used. There is little evidence of a struggle for power as the group operates. The issue is not who controls but how to get the job done.

GROUP SENSITIVITY AND REVIEW

The group is self-conscious about its own operations. Frequently, it will stop to examine how well it is doing or what may be interfering with its operations. The problem may be a matter of procedure, or it may be an individual whose behaviour is preventing the accomplishment of the group's objectives. Whatever the problem is, it is openly discussed until a solution is found.

In pointing out that effective teams are generally self-conscious about the way in which they operate, and so tend to be very much aware when they are providing high performance, the importance of the organisation actually placing a value on this cannot be emphasised too strongly.

All too often within organisations that claim to place a high value on teamwork, it is individual contributions which are recognised. Some examples of this might be "employee of the month" schemes, individual bonuses and using appraisal systems to over-emphasise individual objectives at the expense of the team. These elements undoubtedly play a valuable part in helping organisations to achieve results, and should not be discounted. Those organisations and managers who claim to value effective teamwork, however, need to ensure that their actions match their words and provide ways of valuing teams and individual contribution to the team itself.

Stop and Think

- *What are the success criteria of your organisation?*
- *Is the emphasis on individuals or teams?*
- *How do you reward success?*

5

Conflict

By the end of this chapter you will be able to understand the importance of:

- effective relationships at work
- distinguishing between healthy and unhealthy conflict
- being able to assess the personal and organisational costs of conflict
- being aware of the importance of feedback in handling conflict situations

When you go to work every day carrying your briefcase, you also carry with you another unseen piece of baggage.

Effective relationships at work depend on people's behaviour; however it is the unseen baggage that governs whether that behaviour is constructive and positively helpful towards the relationship or whether it is destructive both on a personal and organisational basis.

The Unseen Baggage

One of the tools which is useful in enabling us to understand our behaviour and the impact that it has on other people is the Strength Deployment Inventory†. This is not a test, it is an instrument which allows individuals to take an inventory of the way in which they use their strengths, and to measure their valued relating style, i.e. the way they prefer to behave in order to feel good about themselves.

† copyright Elias H. Porter and Sara E. Maloney

Within the Strength Deployment Inventory† there are four distinct behavioural patterns which reflect the individual's underlying motivation.

1. **The Assertive Directing Orientation (red)** The value system of these individuals reflects a concern for task accomplishment and the achievement of results.

2. **The Altruistic Nurturing Orientation (blue)** The value system reflects a high level of concern for people and their welfare.

3. **The Analytic Autonomising Orientation (green)** The value system of these individuals reflects a concern for order and self-dependence, for fairness, and the preservation of resources.

4. **The Flexible Cohering Orientation (hub)** The value system of these individuals reflects a concern for the welfare of the group and the exercise of flexibility in pursuing the goals of the group.

Use of the Strength Deployment Inventory† allows people to understand better their own valued relating style and to understand that the individual with a relating style different to their own may see the same situation in a very different way.

The Inventory will also help individuals to understand that as they become defensive in a conflict situation so their behavioural preference will change.

† copyright Elias H. Porter and Sara E. Maloney

Example:
Janet, a reflective independent methodical person was a successful member of an extremely results orientated sales team. Although Janet did well in her job, her colleagues saw her as withdrawn and sometimes nit-picking, whilst she viewed her fellow team members as over aggressive, pushy and arrogant. It was only when this team began to understand the differences in valued relating style and to make the most of the differences rather than allow them to be obstacles that the team began to move towards fulfilling its full potential.

Understanding some of the reasons why people behave in the way that they do, as well as the impact of the organisational environment and the culture on the way that individuals behave in teams, can provide a useful framework to allow conflict to be handled in a positive and constructive way.

If handled in this way conflict can be a source of energy and creativity, leading to generation of new ideas and effective evaluation of existing ideas.

If, however, conflict is handled destructively; either ignored and left to fester or turned into personal attacks, then there can be a high level of organisational cost.

How is conflict handled in your organisation and in your team?
A team in which everyone gets on well together and no disagreements are expressed publicly is not necessarily an effective team.

Irving Janis, an American writer, formulated the concept of "group think" as a way of analysing why poor decisions are often made by teams of extremely bright people. He took the example of the Bay of Pigs, the decision to invade Cuba made by John F. Kennedy's administration. Janis put forward the idea that "group think" occurs when the group is highly cohesive and no-one within it is prepared to challenge either the leader's or their colleagues' ideas. Janis pointed out the paradox that groups of high-minded liberal humanitarian individuals may, in the "group think" situation, take decisions that involve killing or maiming large numbers of people.

Although it is true that in organisational terms the decisions that are taken are less momentous, many decisions that are taken can drastically affect people's livelihoods. The results of "group think" can be seen in the culture of the 1980s and the effect that has had on organisations that are no longer appropriate to the 1990s.

Many organisations that became fixated with diversifi-cations in the 1980s are re-focusing on core business in the 1990s.

It is important to create an atmosphere of openness and trust where issues which are causing conflict can be con-fronted and dealt with so that creative energy can be encouraged and misunderstandings cleared up.

Our experience of enabling existing work teams to examine their own effectiveness has shown that those teams which are the quickest to assert that they do not have any difficult issues to confront are often those which discover, by going through the process of self-examination and team review, that the reality is very different. The team has become stuck in a low-performance rut through a reluctance to bring difficult issues out into the open and confront them in a constructive and positive way.

In some organisations the culture exists where difficult issues are confronted and dealt with at an early stage. Managers have the authority to take decisions to resolve issues quickly without having to pass them up a long decision-making chain. In these organisations a high value is placed on openness and trust is built up over a long period of time. These are organisations in which words and actions are matched. Individuals who are in positions of authority are perceived to be acting authentically so that decisions that are taken, whilst they may not be popular, are generally seen to be in the best interests of the organisation.

In other organisations, however, conflict is perceived as something to be avoided at all costs. This means that frustration and resentment often accumulate, people feel powerless to change anything and back-biting gossip and rumour prevail. In these organisations the reluctance to allow open expression of what people are thinking and feeling about difficult issues means that poor performance is tolerated over long periods of time or dealt with by moving the poor performer to another department.

> In one particular organisation the reluctance to con-
> front poor performance was such that poor performers
> in one job function were moved round 16 different
> locations without any one manager being prepared to
> be open enough with the hapless individuals to tell
> them their performance was not up to standard.

In dealing with conflict we are affected by both organisational environment and our own personal approach. That is, do we meet conflict head on or try to avoid it?

As well as an awareness of your organisation and of your own style it is also important to be aware of the situation. The key questions here are:

- is there an organisational cost?
- can it be quantified?

If the answer to both questions is yes, then conflict must be addressed.

One useful means of assessing openness in a work relationship is to think of it in terms of the Johari Window (Luft and Ingham 1955). The Johari Window is a graphic model of interpersonal relations.

The principle of the Johari Window is that, if you open yourself to others and if you allow others to show you more of yourself, then you enlarge the Open area and all four areas are affected. Through Feedback from others, the size of box 1 is increased and box 2 decreased. Through Self-Disclosure, the size of box 3 is decreased and box 1 is increased. Box 1 represents the open area.

Feedback ⟶

	1	2
Disclosure ↓	Arena	Blind Spot
	Facade 3	4 Un-known

Increasing Awareness

Opening the arena through seeking feedback, or through self-disclosure, does of course involve risk, and creating an atmosphere of trust within the team where people begin to feel that it is safe to take the risk of expressing what they think and feel is one of the key elements of teambuilding that needs to be paid considerable attention.

	KNOWN TO SELF	UNKNOWN TO SELF
	FEEDBACK SEEKING	
KNOWN TO OTHERS	**ARENA** 1 You know and others know (the impression you know you are giving)	**BLIND SPOT** 2 You don't know but others do (the impression you may be giving, unknown to yourself)
UNKNOWN TO OTHERS	**FACADE** 3 You know but others do not (the part of you that you hide)	**UNKNOWN** 4 You don't know and others don't know

(left vertical axis label: **DISCLOSURE**)

The proportions of each area will differ for any individual person, e.g.:

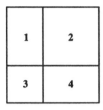

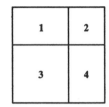

It has become clear to us from our experience of working with teams in many different organisations that opening up the arena either on a one-to-one basis or on a group basis (the first often leads to the second) has very beneficial effects; it clarifies misunderstandings, creates awareness of the different perceptions of others and enables the work relationship to be more effective.

All constructive feedback should be:

- Descriptive (describes the effects of the behaviour rather than labels the person)
- Specific (it should specify exactly the behaviour that is unacceptable)
- Appropriate to the needs of the situation (if we are unlikely to encounter a particular difficult individual again we may decide that it is not worth the effort to provide constructive feedback)
- Focused on behaviour that can be changed or modified
- Asked for rather than imposed (this implies the build up of trust)
- Properly timed so that it is as soon as possible after the event (but has been carefully thought through)

In looking at handling conflict and its likely effects on the team it has been established that:

- confronting issues
- not allowing them to fester
- building openness and trust
- giving appropriate and constructive feedback

are all important elements. This means that in a conflict situation it is better not to rush into the attack straight away, but bear in mind the importance of choosing the right time to actually take some time to consider the best approach to the situation.

The following series of questions provide a useful starting point to consider how you can most constructively handle a situation where interpersonal conflict is involved and there is an organisational cost.

Using this structured questionnaire will enable you to build up a clearer picture of some of the component behaviours in others which can create a conflict situation for you.

In your mind, identify a particular person at work with whom you are in conflict. Imagine this person as concretely as possible.

How do they look? (Dress, style, posture, gestures, face, eyes)

_____

_____

(We tend to judge others according to our values and may sometimes be irrational: "I don't like people with beards", "Have they cleaned their shoes?", "Do they wear a suit?")

What is their predominant attitude towards you? (Kindly, patronising, subservient, pushy)

_____

_____

(Is our perception different from their intention?)

What do you like about this person?

_____

_____

(Find something – it's too easy to say "nothing"!)

What irritates you about this person?

_____

_____

(Be specific and focus on behaviour, not personality)

How are you creative together?

_____

_____

(There must be something – or how might you be creative together?)

How do you frustrate each other?

_____

_____

(NB each other – it's a two way process!)

What kind of things does the other say to make you most irritated?

_____

_____

(Why should this irritate you?)

What kind of behaviours of the other offend you?

_____

_____

(Could it be changed or modified?)

How do you express yourself – your enthusiasm, your irritation, your sympathy, your disagreement, your appreciation of this person?

_____

_____

(Do they perceive it as constructive or destructive?)

Is there an organisation cost due to this conflict situation?
Yes/No
If yes, how would you describe it?

_____

_____

What would you most like to say to this person?

_____

_____

(Be aware of any ways you censor yourself!)

How would you say it?

_____

_____

Stop and Think

- *Do I have a good reason for being open, i.e. do I care enough about the relationship to make it worth the effort?*
- *Am I able to handle openness in the situation sensitively and does it serve not only my needs but also the needs of the other person?*
- *If I take the risk of initiating openness am I prepared for the consequences?*
- *Is the other person likely to be receptive or am I coercing them into openness?*
- *Have I built up enough trust to ensure that the other person feels safe enough to drop some defences of their own accord?*
- *Can I accept that I alone am responsible for my own behaviour and so too are other people responsible for their behaviour?*
- *Am I being realistic about what can be achieved through openness, i.e. a sharing of understanding about the relationship, not a change in the other person's personality?*
- *Am I focusing on "here and now" behaviour and not allowing myself to be side-tracked?*

6

Team Working Trends

In this chapter we will examine the changes – internal and external that have shaped team working in the UK over the last 30 years.

One of the earliest and perhaps most significant trends in team working are to be found in the origins of Team Briefing. Advocated by The Industrial Society as good practice, it can be argued that Briefing laid the foundations for team working.

A communication system, Briefing ensures that every member of every team receives regular, relevant information, in a face-to-face format alongside other members. Briefing groups were introduced in the sixties, primarily as a post-decision making, management – tell mechanism to ensure that staff were informed of and understood management decisions and intentions relating to the workplace.

It is perhaps relevant to reflect on the industrial relations history relating to this and the next decades – in many cases a climate existed where militancy prevailed, a directive approach was required and in some situations managers were striving to exert or regain control over the communication and decision-making process within their organisations.

However, as we have discussed earlier, in the 1990's some different internal and external situations are apparent:

- Workgroups are generally better informed of general and specific issues by management than they were 20-30 years ago. (Many through the use of Briefing.)
- Individuals have a clearer understanding and acceptance of what is expected from them and their contribution to the workgroup. (Use of job descriptions, key result areas, specific targets and appraisal systems have all increased dramatically in the past 20-30 years.)
- The labour market has changed – there is less freedom of movement than before in many sectors and geographic locations, as many traditional areas of work have become less labour intensive.
- Prospects for promotion may disappear; the only viable alternative becomes horizontal job enrichment.
- Potential communication problems involving disparate workgroups over large areas and countries, together with outworking and home-based working, have been largely overcome by technological (advances – electronic mail, fax machines, tele-conferencing and computer modems.
- Generally there is an air of more co-operation and less confrontation.

Consequently the expectations and aspirations of people at work have altered and in many more cases so too has the concept of appropriate leadership style, dependent on group maturity and task requirements. Indeed where there was once a great emphasis on the introduction of downwards appraisal systems, now there is a trend in many organisations to complement this system with an upwards appraisal process. In this review each employee has the right to appraise their boss's management skills. The paperwork can be anonymous if the employee wishes and can be sent in to a central collection area (usually Personnel) where comments are received and summaries passed on to individual managers.

One large organisation that we work with has had an upwards appraisal system for three years and currently 93% of all staff are prepared to identify themselves when completing the form in respect of their boss. This is clearly an indication of a positive attitude of openness and trust, and of their commitment to the organisation itself.

Traditional manager/employee roles are changing in other areas also – areas like decision making and problem solving where the necessary authority and autonomy has been effectively delegated to teams and individuals, leaving them empowered to think for themselves. To achieve this many managers have had to fundamentally alter their own approach to become **less directive, more guiding** and **more enabling**.

Coaching and mentoring skills may have to be learned to facilitate this, and a longer-term vision may have to contest with short-term results.

One consequence of empowerment and autonomy is the concept of the self-managed team. In many organisations this concept is now a reality and in most instances a highly effective reality.

We should look again at the **FORMING – STORMING – NORMING – PERFORMING** process as a continuum along which all teams have to pass prior to achieving a self-managed team profile. (This is the ultimate in situational leadership approach – the best-suited individual for the circumstance has the explicit approval of the rest to select appropriate action.)

We were recently asked to advise one organisation that had recently restructured and as part of the process had designated two groups as self-managing. The restructure was not working out as planned, and on closer investigation two major points were identified:

- The groups had been in the past stuck in the storming phase – indeed trench warfare had become a way of life to most members.
- Individuals had no awareness of the team dynamic process. As a result changes were being experienced with no awareness as to whether they were natural or desirable.

Consequently there was a level of disquiet that had an impact upon the effectiveness of the organisation.

The problem itself was recoverable however, and now six months on, the company is about to introduce a different structure, based on the concept of internal and external customers where each team has identified and set its own objectives (checking first they fit in with the Group five-year plan, and other teams' operating objectives).

In the example on the previous page, the restructuring did not end with team objective-setting however, as each team is now appraised formally bi-monthly by its internal customers on the deliverable performance they have achieved in respect of the objectives.

Back to the Future?

For this organisation, and many others, the concept of team working and high performance teams is a reality.

Other organisations will see it as a risk, or as a new gimmick. We believe it represents not just a fad, but the future, and that the concepts are not new.

> *"It is immoral to misuse people, underuse them and abuse them but it is highly moral to call forth and make use of the talents that are in people. It is also certain that people will not use their gifts to the benefit of the organisation unless they are treated as people with all the needs that people have."*
>
> *(St Thomas Aquinas, 13th Century)*

Bibliography

Management Teams – Why they Succeed or Fail
Belbin, Meredith (Butterworth-Heinemann 1990)

Corporate Cultures
Deal and Kennedy

Gods of Management
Handy, Charles (Pan 1985)

Team Players and Team Work
Parker, Glen (Jossey – Bass Management Series 1990)

Strength Deployment Inventory
Porter, Elias H. (Personal Strengths Publishing Inc. 1973, 1989)

Psychological Testing – A Manager's Guide (2nd Edition)
Toplis, Dulewicz & Fletcher (IPM 1991)

50 Activities for Teambuilding
Woodcock, Mike (Gower 1989)